INFINITE HEALING

Poems and Messages for the Loss of Your Animal Companion

GORMAN POETRY

Copyright © 2022, 2024 Paul J. Gorman
All Rights Reserved

Year of the Book
135 Glen Avenue
Glen Rock, PA 17327

ISBN 13: 978-1-64649-416-3 (print)
ISBN 13: 978-1-64649-417-0 (ebook)

Cover photo: Taken in Western Maryland by the author.

No part of this publication may be reproduced, distributed, or transmitted in any form or by any means, including photocopying, recording, or other electronic or mechanical methods, without the prior written permission of the author, except in the case of brief quotations embodied in critical reviews and certain other noncommercial uses permitted by copyright law.

Library of Congress Control Number: 2022912016

This book explores the stages of grief and resolution in poetry and messages from "Oneness." Seek out a professional grief counselor or pet loss support group (www.aplb.org) who can help facilitate lasting healing as you process your emotions, not compounded by aloneness.

PRAISE FOR GORMAN POETRY

"I wish I'd had Paul Gorman's *Infinite Healing: Poems and Messages for the Loss of Your Animal Companion* when I faced my first painful loss. His words, told in rhyming verse and with compelling sentiment, would have helped ease my sorrow. This book is a real treasure and will have animal lovers weeping again for the loss of their best friends, but weeping in a good way, knowing that these wonderful fur babies will be with us forever in our hearts and throughout eternity in the life hereafter."
—EMILY-JANE HILLS ORFORD

"Written specifically for those who have lost their beloved pet, this short collection is a wonderful tribute to the love our companions have taught us. At first, I feared that this poetry collection might sadden me, and it was a pleasant surprise to find so many words of comfort here. I recommend it to all owners who have lost their dear friends. I am sure they will be as moved and comforted as I have been."
—ASTRID IUSTULIN

"*Infinite Healing* is a beautiful collection of poems about the experience of loving and losing a pet in death. It talks about how to overcome the grief, cope with the pain, and its questions and answers provide solace to the grief-stricken. The poems are short but deeply profound in their simplicity. Gorman's beautiful poetry will bring comfort and perhaps joy in knowing that, in the end, the pet has lived its purpose."
— JENNIE MORE

OTHER WORKS BY THIS AUTHOR

*Poems of Life, Love,
and the Meaning of Meaning*

Poet Gone Wild

Sojourn

The Lightness of Being

*Infinite Healing: Poems and Messages
for the Loss of a Loved One*

Contents

Introduction 1
Message From Oneness 3
As Good As You 4
Truly Alive 5
Do Our Animal Companions Stay Around Us? .. 6
What Do Pets Appreciate Most? 7
I Will Always Miss You 8
Now You Are Free 8
Do Animals Not Need Lessons? 10
What Are Their Most Important Teachings? 11
Love For Me 12
How You Lived 13
Why Don't Animals Live Longer? 14
What Do Animals Feel After Death? 15
One Of Each 16
One Day For Me 17
Did My Pet Choose Me? 18
Do Animals See Death As Natural? 19
More Than Ever 20
Now I Know Why 21
What Do Pets Do After They Die? 22
What Do They See? 23
Please Give Me Some Time 24
My Pet Is At Peace 25

Do Animals Choose The Time Of Their Death? 26
So They Die When They Need To Die? 27
God Sent Me You... 28
Cycles In Time... 29
Will My Pet Send Me A Sign? 30
Could I Get A Glimpse Of My Pet's Spirit?.........31
Still With Me 32
To Be Okay 33
Will My Pet's Spirit Come To Me In Dreams? .. 34
Did My Pet Teach Me Unconditional Love? 35
Pure Love Heals 36
The Purpose Of My Pet's Life 38
Do Animals Hold On To Negative Thoughts? .. 39
No Words 40
We'll Both Be At Home 41
Will I See My Pet Again? 42
That Is Good To Know... 43
Still My Guide... 44
Another Pet To Love 45
Lighted Display 46
You Showed Me The Way 48
You're Still In My Heart...................................... 49
Other Pets In The Home 50
Angels...51
Afterword 52
Postscript.. 54
Glossary...57
Natural Laws 58

INTRODUCTION

I am sorry if your animal companion has passed away. Animals and pets keep us grounded in the present moment, centered on the importance of the simple things in life. Their loving presence is constant, and connects us to God by bringing out the love that we have inside. Expressing love is the primary spiritual function of our being alive, and is especially precious in the modern world of streaming fear and negativity.

Losing this connection can make the grief particularly painful. When our animal companion passes away, the emptiness from their absence can be unbearable in the beginning. Take time to heal. Even in the best-case scenarios, animals do not live long enough–but long enough to teach us about unconditional love, loyalty, patience, courage, honesty with feelings—qualities that will last forever on our healing journeys together, even after we are parted.

Thank God for nature and our animal friends and companions. Know that we are eternally connected to them, and that we will be reconnected when our time on earth is also complete. I hope this book helps lessen the pain of your loss, and highlights the true blessings that life and the animal kingdom give to us.

> *God is the expression in life*
> *as you loving its creatures—*
> *and them loving you, eternally.*

*Animals illuminate in the Mind of God,
illuminating **infinite healing**
in timelessness.*
— Oneness

As Good As You

You would have gladly
   given your life for me
and that's what you did
   I can sadly see

you taught me to love
   and what love will do
now I wish I could be
   half as good as you

Truly Alive

Not afraid of life
    nor afraid of death
not worried about time
    or the time that was left

your spirit inside
    will never die
it came through life
    to be truly alive

    and so was I

Do our animal companions stay around us in spirit after they die?
Yes, allowing them another way to heal their human companions in timelessness.

Are you Oneness?
Allowing the mind an adventure in life's illusion of twoness, yes.

What do pets appreciate most about owners who love them?
Unconditional love in humans includes healing them in time.

What do pets want most out of life?
The loving home that God has promised them in nature, or lesser degrees of living in a home with people.

I Will Always Miss You

The place is so empty
   since you're not here
actually it's full
   of reminders and tears

the opposite of joy
   when you were near
destroyed in a void
   I'll be healing for years

I will always miss you

Now You Are Free

I guess I couldn't
have loved you more
and to know the conditions
of what unconditional's for

what else could it be
love's all I could see
there are no conditions
now you are free

Do animals not need to learn lessons of love and self-love, forgiveness, guilt and shame?
Animals all work to teach humanity more than they learn in their incarnations.

What are their most important teachings?
Allowing flowing of life and loving it in each moment, healing others in time. Unconditionally allowing love, life, and loss of life.
All motion means half healing in life's motion, and half moving and living in gratitude.
All life allows more life and healing in time.

LOVE FOR ME

Patience and courage
and on and on
loyalty and love
    now suddenly gone

please don't leave me
    sad and beyond
only you could relieve
    no need to respond

would you please
    leave these three
patience and courage
    and love for me

How You Lived

I saw how you lived
   and brought out the best
with people you met
   like it was God's request

maybe it was
   and God wanted to see
if you could teach a few tricks
   to an old dog like me

when you see him
   since you passed the test
please tell him I'm trying
   and at last you can rest

Why don't animals live a lot longer?
Loving life means losing life in one last moment of healing into God Mind.
Healing allows life's DNA portals to open, illuminating healed into God Mind.
Nothing heals in darkened portals.

What do animals feel after death?
Loving life—allowing life to end in time, opening in timelessness routinely heals each one infinitely in Oneness.

Do sick and dying pets appreciate when they are assisted in transitioning out of their lives with euthanasia?
Not healing in life means healing in losing life, so yes.

One of Each

You came to teach
   and you loved to be
your time on earth
   so very brief

our time was to reach
   what I will keep
love for me
   and what pure love means

love is peace
   free and released
life is to love
   as one of each

ONE DAY FOR ME

One day for me
   to you is a week
you were slowing down
   I could easily see

I did all I could
   to keep you at ease
and didn't know if I could
   ever help you release

and find relief
   I'm not good with grief
and had always hoped
   you'd find peace in your sleep

the time finally arrived
   and now you are free
in my mind you're alive
   and will always be

now one day for me
   feels like an eternity

Did my pet choose me on a soul level?
Love, life, and losing life all connect in time to heal in timelessness.

Could my pet always know my feelings?
All minds opening in love know each other.

Do animals see death as natural?
All dealing in nature willingly heal in time, or in timelessness—meaning in death.

Are animals afraid of death?
Instincts allow survival; love allows death.

MORE THAN EVER

Always together
 in a pair of two
you were here for me
 and I was there for you

now out of sight
 but not out of mind
I knew in this life
 that I would find

real love and joy
 that lasts forever
and I need it now
 more than ever

Now I Know Why

They said you were stray
   maybe had run away
it was not by chance
   we had met that day

no hope, no home
   I know you were scared
to be alone
   like nobody cared

you deserved love
   and so did I
we are eternally paired
   and now I know why

What do pets do in the spirit world after they die?
Love life, love God, and love themselves.

Do they have spirit bodies and animal consciousness?
All healed in the Mind of God, meaning half in time in life, and half in timeless Oneness—they illuminate in light bodies, healed in timelessness.

What do they see?
People in earth life healing in time or in timelessness into the Mind of God.

Do they see other animals in spirit?
Only their parents and loving mates in the lifetime most recently healed.

So if they have offspring, will they see them in timelessness also?
Not until the lifetime is healed, allowing the offspring to fully heal into the Mind of God. Lifetime introspection allows humans to move toward Oneness willingly. Introspection does not heal animals; they live in the now moment in the Mind of God.

PLEASE GIVE ME SOME TIME

Please give me some time
   to say goodbye
to grieve and to cry
   and to stop asking why

there can't be a loss
   unless something was gained
from all that I know
   your love has remained

your memory is alive
   and cherished inside
I'll be right behind you
   please give me some time

My Pet Is At Peace

What can be said
    when we are bereaved
our beloved pet leaves
    and is now relieved

of physical pain
    and limitation
how do I explain
    their continuation

why did they go
    I know why they came
the love that I know
    is what life has gained

now it is changed
    love will heal my grief
love is free and released
    my pet is at peace

Do our animal companions choose the time of their deaths on a soul level?
Motioning toward Oneness likens to a hopping toy requiring light to hop—losing light in each hop, and gaining light in each healing.
Healing in death creates light, allowing motioning toward Oneness to continue.

So they die when they need to die?
Losing light in time, lighting in timelessness, yes.

Are animals more spiritually advanced than people?
Not more advanced, less mentally capable of losing light in their DNA in negative thinking.

GOD SENT ME YOU

Did you have to go
 and leave me alone
for all that I know
 you had to go home

not what I planned
 or could understand
now in God's hands
 and what life demands

is for me to allow
 receive and accept
forever starts now
 to believe in except

whatever I do
 and I know it is true
that for me to know love
 God sent me you

 thank you God

Cycles In Time

I try to see
   the cycles in time
life's coming and going
   but this time is mine

to understand
   my gain as a loss
how can I be fine
   if pain is the cost

of knowing love
   when life is lost
the difference being
   where both lines cross

leaving me here
   with nowhere to turn
cycles in time
   I may never learn

Will my pet send me a sign that they are still near me in spirit?
All motioning toward Oneness will motion to life in time—meaning healing in the motions of light—light motions healing in the mind, healing creates more light, and so on.

Could I get a glimpse of my pet's spirit moving in my peripheral vision?
Not moving, illuminating in lightness, loving life, allowing healing, and so on.
Life not moving in time is illuminated in timelessness.
Not healing in time illuminates healed in timelessness.
Not healing in timelessness is the healed Mind of God.
Animals are in the Mind of God.

STILL WITH ME

Send me a sign
   I'll feel it inside
in the Mind of God
   you're still alive

infinite and free
   love is still with me
you are by my side
   and will always be

To Be Okay

It's been tough to discover
   that life isn't fair
it's enough to recover
   when I don't care

not in my despair
   life's been taken away
not today
   when I can only say

my companion is gone
   I only hope and pray
that our divine creator
   will show me the way

to live again
   to laugh and to play
and our happy memories
   will always stay

always is forever
   come what may
helping me to heal
   and to be okay

Will my pet in spirit come to me in dreams to bring me peace?
All motioning in light, illuminating in dreams, healing in the mind, yes.
Motion means motioning toward Oneness willingly.

Did my animal companion teach me what unconditional love is?
No, the love healing in your mind allowed your animal to open it, healing the mind.

Pure Love Heals

Pure love means
   only one thing to me
in the overall
  scheme of things

love of God
  and love of life
love of self
  as one despite

when there was fear
  and I had doubt
you were here
  to balance it out

and now I know
  what you came to show
it didn't take long
  before you would go

so I'll try to retain
  what you would teach
to be grounded in now
  and inside I will reach

all that I learned
  and how I could feel
you taught me to allow
  now pure love heals

Was healing my mind the purpose of my pet's life?
All life has one purpose to motion toward Oneness—glowing illuminated in time, or in timelessness.

I hear a bird singing outside. They don't hold onto negative thoughts, do they?
All healing in each moment and each loving song, no.

No Words

Too advanced to speak
love needs no words
I'm alone in my grief
   as I feed the birds

sing me a song
   and let it repeat
sad and sweet
   if you know what that means

but you only know love
   in your songs of joy
and all of life heals
   by hearing your voice

We'll Both Be At Home

I would give
   all I own
for you to live
   and to be back home

I've already lost
   what I really need
and all I want
   is having you with me

now in my heart
   my time to grieve
we'll both be at home
   at my time to leave

Will I see my pet again at the end of my life?
Yes, other pets and relatives will meet you also.

In spirit?
As lightness in the Mind of God.

That is good to know.
All of life knows love in light, and lightness in God Mind.

STILL MY GUIDE

I guess I'll never
   see you again
or maybe I will
   and that will be when

we'll both be alive
   even after we've died
you brought out love
   and I'll say I tried

as long as we're together
   side by side
always and forever
   you are still my guide

Another Pet To Love

Death has come
  when unexpected
nothing can be done
  life is unprotected

just like that
  did life go away
I am the one
  with nothing to say

except that I know
  on one fine day
another pet to love
  you will send my way

LIGHTED DISPLAY

How can a person best heal their grief from the loss of a pet?
Allow one month and then another to pass, accelerating healing over time.
After one month, make a lighted display of pictures in the mind or in the home, healing in the illumination of the display each morning and evening.

Will this heal their grief?
Allow healing in time to lessen the grief. In one year, allow memories of only happy times together, noting the loss only as an incidence of pain in the past, healed into the present.
Life means healing in time, and loving life in each moment.

What color light would be best for illuminating the photo display?
Magenta light in the morning allows healing during the daytime. Light blue light in the evening allows healing in the nighttime.

You Showed Me the Way

"You're so beautiful
   I can hardly stand it"
our bedtime prayer
   and you could understand it

you don't have to speak
   your love I will keep
I could see in your eyes
   as you went off to sleep

I live for the day
   to join you and say
our good night turned to light
   and you showed me the way

You're Still In My Heart

My happiness is in
   a photo display
to light and portray
   I was happy that day

I can't feel it now
   but know and will pray
that more joyful memories
   are coming my way

to make my life
   how I want it to be
just glad inside
   remembering you with me

but now we're apart
   life took you away
you're still in my heart
   where you will always stay

OTHER PETS IN THE HOME

Can other pets in the home see a deceased pet in spirit?
All will heal illuminating in timelessness.
Filaments illuminating in the living pets
allow half knowing, and half feeling another pet
illuminating in timelessness.

Can they see them?
All feeling and knowing illuminates seeing in their minds.
Healing illuminates in time and in timelessness.
Nothing heals in darkness, so animals are healed in their minds in lightness.

ANGELS

What are angels?
All light beings that alternate illumination in Light Mind and God Mind, allowing the Light Mind full healing in God Mind. Angels illuminate the Light Minds losing light.

Is it good to call on angels in life?
A healed mind notices their lightness of being, yes. Call on them to illuminate more of the Light Mind, healing it in God Mind.

Are pets angels?
Only healing lights in the Light Mind of pets, illuminating the life-minds of human companions. Healing the life-mind into the Light Mind is the work of angels, so animal companions do the work of angels. Not healing in the Light Mind means angels need assistance on earth—or from nature, animals, and other people.

Afterword

Do animals go to heaven?
Not heaven, Oneness.

Is that what we would call heaven?
All Oneness healed in God Mind illuminating infinitely, yes.

What about wild animals, fish, or livestock?
Healed in God Mind, illuminating in Oneness—half in time, and half in timelessness—life means loving life, allowing healing in God Mind.

Do animals live in the Mind of God?
All open in the Mind of God.

What does that mean?
Nature illuminates half in time, alternating half in timelessness or God Mind healed.
Not healing in time means life loses light in the life-mind or left brain.
Nature only has one mind, lighting open in God Mind, healed in timelessness.

How can people illuminate in time?
Loving life illuminates in God Mind. Not loving life closes and darkens healing portals in life's DNA—half in time, and half in timelessness.

Do animals and nature teach us to love life?
Allowing healing in God Mind, yes.

Postscript

Please sum up the meaning of life for people in one sentence.
Life heals illuminating in time; love heals infinitely illuminated in timelessness.

So the meaning of life is to heal?
Allowing healing.

By loving life?
And life loving itself healing in you. Not allowing healing in life loses light, closing and darkening portals in DNA.

Do we need to gain light?
"Allow" light in each mind, yes.

How do we allow it?
Loving life means acknowledging Oneness in all things.

What do you mean by "light"?
A healing loving photon particle, local and non-local—healing in time, or healed in timelessness.

Is the point of life to love it?
All heals in loving life and loving itself in it.

All of nature loves life, correct?
Yes, nothing in nature hates life.

So it is up to our left brains to choose in each moment?
Judging means non-judgment.

Kind of like animals?
Animals depend on instincts and not judging.

And they love.
Animals love life, love God, and love themselves.

"For Life is continuous and is Infinite."

—Edgar Cayce

GLOSSARY

Oneness: Infinity healed illuminating in God Mind.

God Mind: All twoness healed and illuminating in Oneness.

Life-mind: Left-brain hemispheres healing and illuminating in an open portal in time.

Light Mind: Right-brain hemispheres opening into the Mind of God.

Light Mind of Godness: Alternating healing and healed in life-mind allowing God Mind.

Portal: An opening in DNA, lighting open in God Mind.

Filaments: Undulating light sensors, halting or allowing light into life through life's DNA.

Light: Life-minds healing half in timelines, and half in timelessness.

Timelessness: All healed in God Mind, not in life-mind.

Time: The lightness of being alternating in the life-mind as the illusion of moving in a progression.

Nature: All of life healing in the Mind of God.

Death: Lighting open healed infinitely in Oneness.

Infinity: All one instant in the Mind of God.

Natural Laws

What if I never
   learned how to talk
only to hear and see
   and to watch with awe

as people stumble
   bumble and mumble
to be silent and humble
   as society crumbles

I would have spoken up
   to point out the flaws
recommend some changes
   show the natural laws

patience and stillness
   I'd stay quiet because
love gives me true courage
   and I walk on my paws

ABOUT THE AUTHOR

Paul Gorman is a
pet owner and rescue donor,
and lives in Frederick, Maryland,
pictured above with Shadow and Dante.

Previous works include: *Poems of Life, Love, and the Meaning of Meaning; Poet Gone Wild; Sojourn; The Lightness of Being*; and *Infinite Healing: Poems and Messages for the Loss of a Loved One.*

email contact: gormanpoetry@gmail.com

www.ingramcontent.com/pod-product-compliance
Lightning Source LLC
Chambersburg PA
CBHW030559080526
44585CB00012B/433